Michael Meier

Philip Jodidio

Richard Meier & Partners

White is the Light

TASCHEN

Illustration page 2 ▶ Richard Meier, 1989
Illustration page 4 ▶ South elevation of the
Hartford Seminary, 1978–81, Hartford,
Connecticut, USA

© 2012 TASCHEN GmbH
Hohenzollernring 53, D-50672 Köln
www.taschen.com

Editor ▶ Peter Gössel, Bremen
Project management ▶ Swantje Schmidt, Bremen
Design and layout ▶ Gössel und Partner, Bremen
Text edited by ▶ Harriet Graham, Turin

Printed in Germany
ISBN 978-3-8365-3853-4

Contents

Introduction

Left page:
Jubilee Church, 1996–2003
Rome, Italy

Whiteness is All

If it is true that Ludwig Mies van der Rohe once said, "God is in the details,"[1] it might be possible to say of Richard Meier's architecture that God is in the numbers. More than any other contemporary architect, Meier has imposed a style that is almost invariably driven by grids and precisely calculated proportions. Nor are these arithmetical elements the only predictable components of his designs. And yet his work is far from being as sterile as its rigorous white demeanor might imply. Why is white, the absence of color, Richard Meier's choice?[2] His own words answer this question best, explain the link between his method and his fundamental concerns, and betray a poetic nature: "White is the ephemeral emblem of perpetual movement. White is always present but never the same, bright and rolling in the day, silver and effervescent under the full moon of New Year's Eve. Between the sea of consciousness and earth's vast materiality lies this ever-changing line of white. White is the light, the medium of understanding and transformative power."[3] Perhaps the most significant word in this description is not "white" but "light." Light floods through the best of Richard Meier's buildings, bringing constant change to his architecture. Clouds moving across the sky, the cycle of the seasons, the arc of the sun, and the moon in the heavens, quintessential expressions of nature, transfigure his grids and white surfaces. Where there is no man-made color, the rising sun and blue sky infuse Meier's forms with the authentic, ephemeral palette of the world. At night, artificial light makes his architecture glow from within, like a lantern in the blackness.

Meier makes no pretense to design "organic" architecture, rather he willfully places his designs in a more reflective context. When asked if his use of white geometric forms might not be considered a symbolic victory over nature, he says, "No. I think that it's really a statement of what we do as architects, that what we make is not natural. I think that the fallacy that Frank Lloyd Wright perpetrated for many years had to do with the nature of materials. He claimed to use what are called natural materials, but the minute you cut down that tree and you use it in construction, it is no longer alive, it is no longer growing, it is inert. The materials we're using in construction are not natural, they do not change with the seasons, or with the time of day. What we make is static in its material quality. Therefore, it's a counterpoint to nature. Nature is changing all around us, and the architecture should help reflect those changes. I think it should help intensify one's perception of the changing colors of nature, changing colors of the day, rather than attempt to have the architecture change."[4]

Light is Life

Richard Meier, born in Newark, New Jersey, in 1934, has been one of the most consistent of contemporary architects, to a point that his stylistic choices, from white aluminum panels to nautical railings, are among the most recognizable of his profession. Beneath these surface elements, Meier's plans continue to call on a geometric vocabulary, often based on the circle and the square. Linking plan to volume, a rigorous system of grids,

1 Ludwig Mies van der Rohe, speaking about restraint in design, in the *New York Herald Tribune*, June 28, 1959.
2 White is not a color, but rather the combination of all the colors of the visible light spectrum. It is sometimes described as an achromatic color, like black.
3 Richard Meier, "Preface", *Richard Meier Architect, 1985/1991*, Rizzoli, New York, 1991.
4 Interview with Richard Meier, Los Angeles, May 16, 1994.

Alvin Ailey, collage, 1998

even more than the choice of white cladding, constitutes the signature element of a Richard Meier building. His is a space where light is an omnipresent element that itself forms the environment, where the architecture creates a feeling of well-being, or of unspoken connection to the natural world, which may, at its best, attain a spiritual dimension. In the words of the architect's friend, the artist Frank Stella, "Light is life."

Richard Meier's own interest in art, expressed in his sculptures or collages, but also, most significantly, in his architecture, is an important element in understanding both his approach and his built work. As the definitions of the word "art" have become more and more complex, often including forms of expression that are far less intellectually and culturally demanding than architecture, the critic is tempted to agree with Meier's appraisal of his own work. In a different time and place, John Ruskin said, "No person who is not a great sculptor or painter *can* be an architect. If he is not a sculptor or painter, he can only be a *builder*."[5] When asked if he makes a fundamental distinction between architecture and art, Meier responds, "No, architecture is just as much a work of art as any other. I make a distinction between architecture and collages of course. I think that there is a problem today in the world. Architecture as an art is a forgotten art. People look at sculpture and painting, but not at architecture. Maybe it has to do with the education of art historians."[6]

Recent architecture and art have been marked by frequent stylistic shifts, or perhaps more accurately by dissolution of style in favor of trends or personal expressions. As the first decade of the 21st century draws to a close with no dominant aesthetic view, the very idea of style has been called into question. Architecture, once a symbol of permanence, has wavered between willful impermanence and computer-generated extravagance. Few mature creators have passed through this period without being tempted by one or another of the fashions of the times. Fewer still have set and maintained a clear course. In fact, an architect or an artist with a style recognizable over the years is exposed to accusations of immobility or inability to change. Yet many of the most durable works of art were born of rules as strict as the unity of time and place of the classical theater. Few would argue that Shakespeare's adherence to Elizabethan parameters prevented him from encompassing the entire range of human experience in his plays. In *King Lear*, the English master wrote, "Ripeness is all."[7] It would be overly simplistic to say that in Meier's case whiteness is all, and yet there is a sense that the life of his art is in the light that plays across his walls or floors. It is precisely its whiteness that allows Richard Meier's architecture to live and breath.

In the Realm of the Masters

Richard Meier attended Columbia High School in Maplewood, New Jersey, a peaceful suburban town, and went on to Cornell University in 1952. Meier has said that "Cornell was very free and open without any dominant influence, and I think that that was the good thing about it. It was left up to the students and what they were interested in to take advantage of a wide variety of opportunities for learning."[8] A literature course taught by Vladimir Nabokov, and lectures by Alan Salomon—who was later to become the director of the Jewish Museum in New York—on Matisse and Picasso seem to have particularly marked him. Subsequent to his graduation from Cornell, Meier traveled through Europe, and had occasion to meet Le Corbusier in France. This early admiration for the Swiss-born master would seem to justify the frequent comparisons made between Meier's own work and that of Le Corbusier. As he said himself years later, "I

5 John Ruskin (1819–1900), British art critic and author. *Lectures on Architecture and Painting*, 61, addenda (1853).
6 Interview with Richard Meier, New York, April 20, 1999.
7 William Shakespeare, "Gloucester. Nor further, sir, a man may rot even here.
Edgar. What, in ill thoughts again? Men must endure Their going hence, even as their coming hither; Ripeness is all." *King Lear*, 5.2, ll.8–11.
8 Richard Meier in Roberto Einaudi, *Richard Meier, Frank Stella, The Work of Richard Meier: Origins and Influences*, Arte e Architettura, Electa, Milan, 1993.

could obviously not create the buildings I do without knowing and loving the work of Corb. Le Corbusier has been a great influence on my mode of creating space."

Cleanness and Bareness and Spareness

Joseph Rykwert relates aspects of an early Meier structure, the Smith House (Darien, Connecticut, 1965–67), to Le Corbusier's Villa Stein (Garches, France, 1927–28), but its play of geometric forms might also bring to mind earlier designs by Theo van Doesburg or Gerrit Rietveld. What is astonishing is the number of characteristics of later Meier buildings that are already apparent in the Smith House. Although the cladding is wood rather than the metal panel that appeared in later buildings, there is a bridge to approach the entrance, a closed façade on the entry side, an open one facing the water, and a high, generously glazed living room. White is already Richard Meier's choice in the mid-1960s for emphasizing the space and light of the Smith House. That white also brought to mind that the purism of Le Corbusier was certainly not an unintentional co-incidence, though some associated Meier's clean geometric vocabulary with the *tabula rasa* of Bauhaus Modernism. The very fact that such varied references to earlier architecture are made in the case of Richard Meier seems to prove that from the beginning of his career he was consciously open to a wide range of influences. Meier explains his point of view in the debate about sources, and pleads in favor of an analysis based more on space than on historic references. "Modernism," he says, "doesn't have to throw out the baby with the bath water. I don't think that everything has to be conceived as being new and different just for difference's sake. I believe that architecture is related to the past, that the present is related to the past, and that we learn from the past in order to move into the future. Clearly that doesn't mean that everything that is past has no meaning. I think that there are ways of dealing with space which we can learn from; I would like to think that I can learn from Bernini and Borromini and Bramante, as well as I can from Le Corbusier, Frank Lloyd Wright and Aalto. This is what's different about modern architecture today and modern architecture as it grew up in the 1930s and 1940s. What we do is related to the history of architecture. What we do is also unfortu-

Chaise Lounge by Richard Meier, 1978–82
Produced by Knoll International

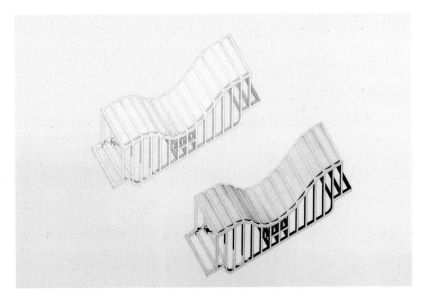

9 Interview with Richard Meier, Los Angeles, May 16, 1994.
10 Tom Wolfe, *From Bauhaus to Our House*, Farrar Straus Giroux, New York, 1981.

nately related to many pragmatic concerns, which don't change overnight either, and ultimately it's a way in which we make space and deal with the making of space. That's what is important in architecture, not so much the references that might occur."9

Among the early public projects of Richard Meier, the Bronx Developmental Center in New York (1970–77) stands out because it represents one of his first large-scale uses of aluminum panels. Intended for physically disabled and mentally retarded children, the Center is located in an industrial area between the Hutchinson River Parkway and railroad tracks. As such, it was difficult to imagine a building that opened out into the environment. Rather, Meier chose to close the outside façades in favor of internal courtyards. The reflective aluminum finish of the wall surfaces indeed seems to contribute to the closed appearance of the building. Another difference between this building and later Meier projects is that the rigorous grid patterns toward which he evolved afterwards seem to be less present. The panels in the Bronx Developmental Center adopt several different formats according to the circumstances, with a full unit measuring 12 x 11 feet (3.7 x 3.3 meters). Although sizable, housing 380 patients together with outpatient facilities, the Bronx Developmental Center brought Richard Meier less notoriety than much smaller individual houses, such as the one he built in Harbor Springs, Michigan, between 1971 and 1973.

The Douglas House owes at least part of its celebrity to its dramatic setting on a steep, wooded site on the shores of Lake Michigan. Related in its design to the Smith House, this home is entered through a bridge at roof level, and in many ways brings naval metaphors to mind. The Douglas House is a strikingly incongruous object in this natural setting, a gleaming white jewel shining in the forest. A decade later, the author Tom Wolfe looked on the popularity of buildings like this one and wrote, "Every new $900 000 summer house in the north woods of Michigan or on the shore of Long Island has so many pipe railings, ramps, hob-tread metal spiral stairways, sheets of industrial plate glass, banks of tungsten-halogen lamps and white cylindrical shapes, it looks like an insecticide refinery. I once saw the owners of such a place driven to the edge of sensory deprivation by the whiteness and lightness and leanness and cleanness and bareness and spareness of it all. They became desperate for an antidote, such as coziness and color."10

Museum of Television and Radio, 1994–96
Beverly Hills, California, USA

You Don't Learn about Architecture from Las Vegas

While the Douglas House was under construction, in 1972 Meier was included in a book entitled *Five Architects*, together with Peter Eisenman, Michael Graves, John Hejduk, and Charles Gwathmey. Their work had already been featured in a 1967 exhibition organized at the Museum of Modern Art (MoMA) in New York by Arthur Drexler, and the architect Philip Johnson, founder of the Department of Architecture and Design at MoMA (1930), surely played an influential role in this grouping. Formalist in its ideas, often compared to the Minimalist artists of the period, this group was quickly attacked by such architects as Robert A. M. Stern who excoriated Colin Rowe for being "stuck in the hothouse aesthetics of the 1920s." Meier's rallying call of the time was, "You don't learn about architecture from Las Vegas," a specific reference to Robert Venturi's influential 1972 book *Learning from Las Vegas*, sequel to the 1966 manifesto *Complexity and Contradiction in Architecture*, which championed "inclusion" and such diverse influences as highway signs and Tom Wolfe's own *Kandy-Colored Tangerine-Flake Streamline Baby*, as opposed to the spare whiteness of the newly baptized "New

York Five." Indeed, much of the debate at this time was led by theoreticians such as Venturi or Peter Eisenman, who had very few, if any, built works to their credit. Graves and Hejduk did more drawing than building, and, curiously, that fact seemed to confer all the more prestige on them, as opposed to the architects who actually "got their hands dirty." On both sides of this theoretical argument, which opposed a certain type of Modernism to the proponents of Postmodernism, there seems to have been much more concern about visual or formal values than a real analysis of the role of architecture in society. The sociological foundations of the modern movement were in any case set aside in favor of matters of aesthetics.

The Idea of Place

Richard Meier's architecture took a clear step forward with his design for the Atheneum in New Harmony, Indiana (1975–79). It is here, at the entrance to the best known utopian community in America, that his vocabulary and style began to be defined in terms of public architecture. Splendidly isolated and elevated because of the danger of flooding along the Wabash River, this building again uses a nautical vocabulary, with its prominent nautical railings and its elegant gangplank-style entrance ramp. It is an ark of culture and precision in a largely natural environment, but, within, there are constant opportunities to see and admire the exterior. Confirming his analysis of the relationship between architecture and nature, he says, "I've defined a vocabulary of forms which I think are not forms one would find in nature. I think that it's very difficult, if not impossible, to make forms as beautiful as those that occur in nature. Nature does it better, but what we can do is to conceive forms which are interrelated in a way, and which may not be interrelated in nature. I think that is really what I am trying to do. I am trying to find a form of construction which has some meaning in human terms, and relates to the idea of the place."[11]

11 Interview with Richard Meier, Los Angeles, May 16, 1994.

Ara Pacis Museum, 1996–2006
Rome, Italy

A complex repertory of the influences that have played on Meier, together with his own areas of predilection, are united in the High Museum of Art in Atlanta, Georgia (1980–83). Like the Atheneum, it has a long entry ramp, but here the defining volume is undoubtedly the monumental atrium. Having worked on the small Aye Simon Reading Room (1977–78) at the Guggenheim, Meier had undoubtedly had time to reflect on the strengths and weaknesses of Wright's defining architectural statement. "I learned from the Guggenheim Museum," says the architect, "where you see a work, and then you go around to the other side of the ramp, and when you look across you see it differently." Although the High Museum does indeed offer multiple points of view on the works of art exhibited, it avoids the problems created by Wright's spiral gallery by separating ramps from galleries. "To some extent the light-filled atrium space is inspired by, and a commentary on, the central space of the Guggenheim Museum," concludes Meier. Expanding on the repertory of curved and rectilinear volumes he had already employed in other projects, Meier defined the atrium of the High Museum as a social gathering place, or cultural center, for the southern city. And yet this definition of gathering implies that the building is turned in on itself. The ramp is an invitation extended to passersby, but any gathering must take place in the building's center. Here, as in other instances, Richard Meier buildings have taken on the appearance of inviolable bastions of perfection, removed from their surroundings, at least as seen from the outside. Although it would be difficult to suggest that his light-flooded volumes project an image of sterility, their perfection, indeed their very whiteness, seem to set them apart from the disorder of existence. "I think that the responsibility of an architect," says Richard Meier, "is really to create a sense of order, a sense of place, a sense of relationships. These ideas are inherent in the architecture, and therefore the precision, or the relationships, are very important to me in making the ideas and the relationships as clear as possible, and in creating a sense of order. I'm not interested in creating chaos; others can do that."[12]

And then Rotate it by 3.5°

Meier's sense of order remains a prominent feature of the projects he undertook in Europe beginning in the late 1970s. It would seem, though, that the richness of the architectural environment of the old Europe inspired him in new ways and obliged him to address the issue of the context of his architecture in a different way than in his earlier work. The first significant example of this trend is the Museum for the Decorative Arts built along the banks of the Main River in Frankfurt, Germany (1979–85). The site is situated on the Museumsufer, on the bank of the river opposite the modern downtown area, and includes the 19th-century Villa Metzler. Using the vocabulary that had by now become his trademark, Richard Meier chose to enter into a close dialogue with this bourgeois house, to surprisingly successful effect. He employed the cubic volume of the Villa to determine the 57.7-foot (17.6-meter) width and height of each quadrant of his grid. Rotating part of the museum structure by 3.5°, he emphasized the alignment of the river embankment as opposed to that of the original house. An internal ramp and numerous openings permit a constant evolution of the points of view of the visitor, along the lines of the High Museum, but without the central atrium. As though to prove that his buildings are more than isolated jewels, he links the Villa Metzler to the new museum via a glass bridge, creating quite a natural connection, despite the radical difference in styles. Finally, the omnipresent white of his architecture here becomes an echo of the past that is far removed from Le Corbusier's purism. Rather, it

12 Interview with Richard Meier, Los Angeles, May 16, 1994.

brings to mind the very German Baroque churches that he had gone to visit from Rome in 1973, when he said, "There is a sense of the spiritual in the use of light in all of the great Baroque churches. There, light is central to the experience of the architectural volume; certainly I have used light to a similar end."

Silver and Effervescent Light of the Moon

The Grotta House (Harding Township, New Jersey, 1984–89) is located on a sloping 2.5-hectare plot of meadowland, surrounded only at a distance by neo-Colonial-style farms. It may be that the purity of Richard Meier's buildings inspires some owners, but the Grottas could be considered almost ideal clients. A childhood friend of Meier's, Mr. Grotta chose the precise location of the house, on top of a gentle hill, with the architect. Well after the completion of the house, its owners insisted that every detail be maintained in perfect condition, and stray objects seemed to be banned from sight. The Grottas' sense of the priority of the architecture made him go so far as to reject the idea of any kind of *brise-soleils* in the cylindrical living room area. Undoubtedly applying the lessons learned in his museums, Richard Meier designed his sixteenth house to permit 360° viewing of the owners' unusual collection of popular art and pottery. Rigorous and relatively simple in its design, the Grotta House offers unexpected surfaces in a Meier building, such as gray enamel paneling and large wall surfaces toward the kitchen and rear in ground-faced concrete block. Grotta marveled at the way this house lives in different types of light, from the rising sun to the brightness of a full moon.

Big in Paris

Designing for large corporations can undoubtedly be as frustrating for an architect as a municipal commission, but Richard Meier's international reputation, reinforced by his 1984 Pritzker Prize, and the RIBA Gold Medal which he received in 1989, has been such that he has often been able to work in privileged circumstances. This was in many

Royal Dutch Paper Mills Headquarters, 1987–92
Hilversum, The Netherlands

ways the case of his Canal+ Headquarters building in Paris (1988–92). At the time one of the most profitable private cable television companies in the world, Canal+ under the leadership of André Rousselet wanted to make an architectural "statement" with its new building, and Richard Meier seemed the logical choice for a forward-looking design. In 1981, Meier had already designed an unbuilt office complex for the automobile manufacturer Renault, destined to occupy a site not far from the Quai André Citroën, where the Canal+ building was then erected. Built in a very short time span, between April 1990 and the end of 1991, it is not blessed with a very good site, set back from the Right Bank of the Seine, near a good deal of mediocre modern architecture and relatively far from the historic city center. The only positive element in the immediate vicinity is the recent André Citroën Park and of course the river itself. And yet Richard Meier has said, "I like to think of this building as Parisian in feeling, intellectual yet sensual, and beautiful in its rationality. Spatially it is simple, but technically it is complex. The building's sheer wall becomes the placard both for Canal+ and its urban presence. Its image from the Seine is of a great ship whose only movement is the changing light."

In the Birthplace of Einstein

During the later part of the 1980s, Richard Meier, like many other American architects, received few commissions in the United States, aside from the enormous Getty Center. This was largely a question of economic circumstances. The recession, though, did not strike continental Europe as early as it did the United States, and after the Frankfurt Museum for the Decorative Arts Meier's reputation in Germany was well established. Just two years after the Frankfurt building was completed, in 1986 he was awarded the daunting task of building on what the German press has called "one of the most problematic sites in the country," the Ulm Münsterplatz. A small city of 100000, the birthplace of Albert Einstein, Ulm saw 85% of its old section destroyed by bombing in 1944. Circumstances after the war there were such that no real effort was made to reconstitute the traditional architecture, as had been the case in Munich, for example. Rather, cheap, modern structures proliferated right up to the large square in front of Ulm Münster, a Lutheran cathedral, one monument that surprisingly escaped Allied bombs all but unscathed. At just over 525 feet (160 meters) in height, the single spire of the cathedral is the tallest of its kind, exceeding that of Cologne, which is a much larger city. Completed only between 1884 and 1890, the spire was the last element of construction, which had begun in 1377. It was designed for 20000 persons, when Ulm had only 10000 inhabitants, and, to this day, its mass is somewhat disproportionate to the city. Nor were bombs and exaggerated ambitions the only problems of this site. Until the 19th century, a Barefooted Friar's monastery and church occupied a large part of the square in front of the cathedral, but these were demolished in 1874–75 to allow a clear view of the spire. Over a period of 105 years, the city launched no fewer than 17 design competitions to fill the space left by the monastery. Until 1987, the site was occupied by a low, undistinguished tourist office and parking area. The 38000-square-foot (3500-square-meter) three-story complex of the Stadthaus built by Richard Meier was dedicated on November 12, 1993, and represents one of his greatest accomplishments, especially given the difficult circumstances involved.

Elegant and Timeless

By far the largest project undertaken by Richard Meier, the Getty Center in Los Angeles

City Hall and Central Library, 1987–95
The Hague, The Netherlands

(1984–97), has done much to define his reputation. A remark that he made about this 947000-square-foot (88000-square-meter) six-building complex situated on a 110-acre (44.5-hectare) hilltop site in the course of design work certainly signals that it stands apart both literally and figuratively in his oeuvre: "In my mind's eye I see a classic structure, elegant and timeless, emerging, serene and ideal, from the rough hillside, a kind of Aristotelian structure within the landscape. Sometimes I think that the landscape overtakes it, and sometimes I see the structure as standing out, dominating the landscape; the two are entwined in a dialogue, a perpetual embrace in which building and site are one. In my mind I keep returning to the Romans, to Hadrian's Villa, to Caprarola for their sequence of spaces, their thick-walled presence, their sense of order, the way in which building and landscape belong to each other." The reference to Caprarola, the Palazzo Farnese, built by Giacomo da Vignola (1507–73) near Viterbo from 1559 to 1573, is rather unexpected. The very rare pentagonal plan of this palace, laden with occult symbolism, and its rather forbidding exterior, dominating the town, seem quite distant from the grace and light of the Ulm Stadthaus. In fact, the Getty Center, unlike almost any other Meier structure, is not entirely white. Due to a Los Angeles law, and a draconian "Conditional Use Permit" that specifically provided that the buildings could not be white, the architect was obliged to seek another solution for the cladding. His choice, cleft travertine from Italy, represents a radical departure from any of the smooth surfaces chosen by him in the past. Its surface is rough, and the thick panels are intentionally hung on the façades in an uneven way. Rather than Meier's usual inviolate perfection, these strong retaining walls, on a very steep site, call to mind images of Greek or Roman ruins. "That's good," responded Meier in 1994. "The Getty is an institution which is related to Greek and Roman culture certainly. The major portion of Mr. Getty's collection was Greek and Roman sculpture, and the design of the original building in Malibu was based on a reconstruction of what the Villa dei Papiri in Herculaneum might have looked like. So if my architecture has that quality, then perhaps it is all the more appropriate for the Getty."[13]

The complex layout of the Getty Center is due to the mountainous terrain, and also to the desire of the client to divide its various departments: the Museum, the Getty Center for the History of Art and the Humanities, the Getty Conservation Institute, the Getty Art History Information Program, the Getty Center for Education in the Arts, and the Getty Grant Program. "The six buildings of the Center have to serve perhaps a dozen purposes," Meier said during the design process. "And yet this complex has to be something more than individual, disparate entities. There must be a sense of the Getty Center. Each building will have its own identity, but each must be a part of the whole." The architect approached this series of problems by creating a plan that bears some comparison to that of Hadrian's Villa at Tivoli. Given the frequent references made by Richard Meier to the architecture of the past and to his own predilection for rotated grids, which often correspond to the axial arrangements of ancient complexes such as the ruins at Tivoli, this connection should not be a real surprise. It does appear here most clearly, however, that Richard Meier is a thoroughly modern architect who feels a deep affinity with the past, be it of this century, or earlier still. When asked why he has related the plan so closely to that of Hadrian's Villa, Meier, insisting that rotated grids are at the heart of the design, replies, "I don't think it's a relationship to a monument. I think it's really an expression of permanence. The Getty is an institution of a certain solidity and permanence."[14]

13 Interview with Richard Meier, Los Angeles, May 16, 1994.
14 Ibid.

Model of the Getty Center, 1991–93
Los Angeles, California, USA

Upside-Down Shed

With the Neugebauer House (Naples, Florida, 1995–98), Richard Meier succeeded in renewing the vocabulary of his residential structures. In an unexpected turn, the architect makes an indirect reference to shed design in a building that is otherwise far separated from an industrial vocabulary. "That's right," says Richard Meier, "this was a very unusual situation in many respects. This was a client coming from abroad who wanted a house in Florida. He had fewer demands than most clients put on a house. The program was on one piece of paper. It was compressed, it was simplified. It was without a lot of encumbrances. There is a rather odd building code in this area which demanded a sloped roof house with a certain one to twelve proportion. We weren't going to do a house that had a pitched roof in the normal sense, so we turned it upside down. It followed the law to the letter, but then we had to say, how do we make it work?"[15] The asymmetrical, V-shaped roof is indeed the defining architectural element of the Neugebauer House, but as always, and perhaps more than elsewhere, Meier has used generous glazing literally to flood the house with light. Clearly the architect is at ease with constraints—those imposed by his own choice of vocabulary as well as those that spring from a site or local building regulations. The very idea of inverting the roof of the Neugebauer House might not have occurred to other architects, and, as surprising as this form remains, it is fundamentally faithful to Richard Meier's constant efforts to innovate within his own chosen range of options.

15 Interview with Richard Meier, New York, April 20, 1999.

That's What You Want—Space and Light

Another exercise in openness, defined in a rather different way, has marked Richard Meier's career since the turn of the century. His series of condominium apartment buildings on Manhattan's West Side (173/176 Perry Street, New York, New York, 1999–2002; 165 Charles Street, New York, New York, 2003–06) has had a profound impact on the design of such structures in the city. Whereas promoters had the impression that it was not worth associating 'name' architects like Richard Meier with condominiums, the architect has proven that his design had a marked effect on property values, and, in a more subtle sense, on the architectural quality of the community. What exactly did his skill bring to the project? "We began Perry Street and then Charles Street," he responds. "We studied the permissible zoning. In New York City, it's basically a wedding cake, though the precise dimensions vary according to the street or area of the city. You can apply for a variance for hardship or any number of different reasons that usually delay the project two or three years. It seemed to me foolhardy to try to do something that was not within the zoning envelope because of the cost, the time, and the neighborhood. So we decided to do the best building we could within the zoning envelope. That meant going up a certain height and that's it. No setbacks. We lost a little bit of what could be considered the maximum square footage. We gave up some ground-floor space to the public—plaza space. It made a sort of a gateway from the West Village toward the park on the Hudson. On Charles Street it really makes a place." Part of the impact of Meier's intervention has to do with the fact that he has been able to group more than one structure in a circumscribed area. "Having three buildings together is very different from doing a single building, because somehow there is a synergy that is created by the activity of the three buildings," he explains.

Elegy in Rome

Despite building in New York, Richard Meier has certainly not given up his ongoing love affair with Europe. His Jubilee Church (1996–2003) was the first Roman structure to be completed. As he points out, the completion of this project marked something of a milestone because it is exceedingly rare, if not unheard of, for the Catholic Church to call on a Jewish architect to design a church, and, at that, one of considerable symbolic importance in this case. The sail-like forms of the church and, indeed, its plan cannot be described as typical in any sense. And yet, here again, Meier has been faithful to his driving geometric instincts. The proportional structure of both the church and the precinct is predicated on a displaced square and four circles. The three shells that determine the primary gestalt of the church are based on three circles of equal radius and refer discreetly to the Holy Trinity. For all of his whiteness, Richard Meier shows with the Jubilee Church that he is capable not only of creating a humane space, but also one that is predictably suffused with light. Aside from the obvious theological references to light that might be invoked, his Roman design speaks with the simplicity and directness of a passing cloud. Light brings it to life and fills its sails with the breath of the divine.

Corb, Mies, and Meier

As the 20th century drew to a close, the rise of a certain minimalism in architecture caused some to restate the influence exerted by significant figures of modern architecture. Terry Riley, the former Chief Curator of the Department of Architecture and Design at MoMA, made pointed reference to the fact that the New York Five had sought their influence in the work of Le Corbusier, but that in the final analysis it was another 20th-century architect who had exerted the greatest influence—Ludwig Mies van der Rohe. When asked about this shift in the understanding of recent architecture, Richard Meier responded in 1999, "Whether it is the influence of Mies or the search for greater simplification, which is certainly what we personified, I think that it is there. We are going toward a simplification of ideas and expressions rather than the kind of layering of meanings that was prevalent in the last decade." And yet the observer of Meier's architecture might well conclude that much of what he embodies is precisely an overlaying of meanings. "Yes," says Meier, "but there is an attempt to not make it so much of an overlay that things get lost. The influence of Mies is an attempt toward a simplification. I am not looking to Mies, but I am looking to a simplification. I remember that I did a house in the late 1960s. This small house was based on a small square and an overlaid grid. I realized that trying to do this in such a small house was just too complicated. It was a good lesson to me. There is a hierarchy that one has to establish. That hierarchy has to be clearly established before you can establish the secondary and tertiary readings. In architecture it is not that easy to get the first reading across."[16]

The point here is not necessarily to trace the relative importance of Le Corbusier and Mies, but rather to understand Meier's own evolution. It seems, as he puts it, that he has been "looking to a simplification" for some years. The clean, clear lines of the lower West Side condominiums retain the feeling of a Meier building without the kind of overworked complexity seen in such buildings as the Royal Dutch Paper Mills Headquarters. The luxurious Neugebauer House traces its lineage to the industrial shed, one of the most basic (and simple) building types. Although it may not be obvious in his careful work, Meier's own, more recent explanation of what he is trying to achieve, is of interest. "I am trying to approach the current work with a less rigorous attitude, letting things be a little looser in a way ... Things can relate, everything being on the grid as it were and trying to see how it can overlap, creating different readings on things."[17] It is true that a gesture like the inverted roof of the Neugebauer House also reveals a new ability to relax the rules.

Where certain forms of Modernism were set aside because of their aridity and lack of concern for inhabitants, Richard Meier has undertaken no less than a rehabilitation of the Modern. His jewel-like buildings, and even his "Italian hill town" above the San Diego Freeway, speak to concerns that are timeless. Without attributing a spiritual dimension to his work that he does not necessarily claim, one can recall the words of the Gospel of Saint Matthew: "A city that is set on a hill cannot be hid. Let your light so shine before men..." The permanence in Richard Meier's buildings may conversely be what is most ephemeral, the passing light, the view toward the Pacific Ocean from the Getty Center's Brentwood hill. "Between the sea of consciousness and earth's vast materiality lies this ever-changing line of white. White is the light, the medium of understanding and transformative power," said Meier many years ago. Art, when it deserves that name, speaks the language of the unspoken. Richard Meier's architecture at its best is built of light and the changing colors of the sky.

16 Interview with Richard Meier, New York, April 20, 1999.
17 Interview with Richard Meier, New York, November 7, 2006.

Sandra Day O'Connor United States
Courthouse, 1994–2000
Phoenix, Arizona, USA

1965–1967 · Smith House
Darien, Connecticut, USA

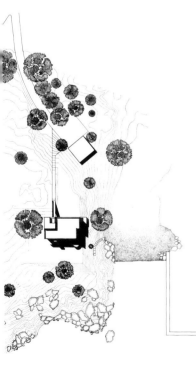

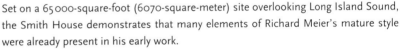

Set on a 65000-square-foot (6070-square-meter) site overlooking Long Island Sound, the Smith House demonstrates that many elements of Richard Meier's mature style were already present in his early work.

Although clad in wood, the house is white. Like many of his later houses, it has a rather closed entrance façade and a generously glazed garden or seaside elevation. The site is marked by a group of pines near the entrance, and drops off to the rock shore and a sandy cove. A division of public and private spaces is made according to the scheme already visible in the exterior façades. The entrance side corresponds to the private zone of the house. As the architect states, "A series of closed, cellular spaces, these private areas are organized through three levels behind an opaque façade, which is intermittently pierced with windows." Visitors are greeted with a dramatic view of the sea and the painted brick fireplace. Three levels of public space are grouped behind the glazed and articulated seaside façade with its central white chimney. The use of ample windows and white surfaces amplifies the impression of changing light that moves through the house with the changing hours and seasons.

Despite his use of the Modernist vocabulary, Richard Meier gives this house a sense of comfort, space, and above all light, which seems quite far removed from the functionalist rigor of the European masters who first gave rise to Modernism. He plays on the volume and on light in an orchestrated manner that decidedly announces his future work.

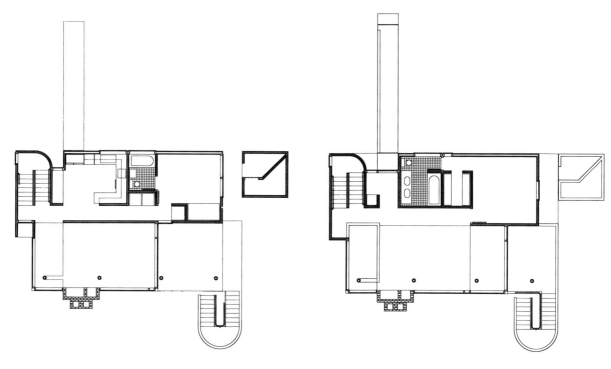

1967–1969 ▸ Saltzman House
East Hampton, New York, USA

With the Saltzman House, Richard Meier continued to attain some of the sculptural and painterly qualities that are the hallmarks of his style. In his own description of the residence, the architect writes, "From a distance, the cubic composition appears to flatten into a two-dimensional shape against the background of land and sky."

Entirely white like its antecedents, the structure is located on 3 acres (1.2 hectares) of flat land looking out to Montauk Point and the Atlantic Ocean. Since the site is slightly inland, the view of the Ocean is accentuated from the two upper levels, and indeed the shoreline cannot be seen from the ground floor. Private sections of the residence are located in two adjacent sides of the structure, but the public space rises through the volume and "opens up like a funnel so the integrity of the private zone is partially eroded on the second level and then disappears entirely on the third."

An outside spiral stair, and a bridge connecting to a small guesthouse, together with distinctive white railings reminiscent of ship design, all confirm the evolving complexity and evolution of Meier's work towards a hieratic style, strictly geometric without being repetitive, filled with the movement and colors of light. Though its geometric articulations and layering may well link it to the experiments of the De Stijl movement (1917–31) as represented in the work of Gerrit Rietveld or even Piet Mondrian, Meier's insistent whiteness also brings to mind such works as Kasimir Malevich's 1918 *Suprematist Composition, White on White.*

1969–1971 ▸ Old Westbury House
Old Westbury, New York, USA

The Old Westbury House is located on a large wooded site that shields it from neighboring roads entirely. On a larger scale than previous work by Meier, it was designed for a family with six children, giving rise to "an unusually large number of bedrooms and bathrooms." A meadow and a pond near the house emphasize the bucolic nature of the site, and the architect again differentiates the more closed front façade from the dramatic glazed elevation facing the pond, just as he divides public and private space inside. This orientation naturally allows for views outward, and permits morning sunlight into the bedrooms.

The suspension of one volume with band windows on thin pilotis might bring to mind Le Corbusier's Villa Savoye (Poissy, France, 1928–29). An internal ramp confirms this impression since this is another feature that the Old Westbury House shares with the masterpiece by Le Corbusier. Clearly on a larger scale than the Poissy house, Meier's design is something of an evolutionary jump away from the past rather than any attempt to imitate Le Corbusier. Light suffuses the Old Westbury House, not only through the vertical glazing, but also from a third-floor skylight that "admits a column of natural light that bisects the axis of the circulation spine." If Richard Meier is an heir of the early Modernists, he is a willful one who plays on his knowledge and seeks to use references such as the Villa Savoye as starting points for his own explorations of space and light.

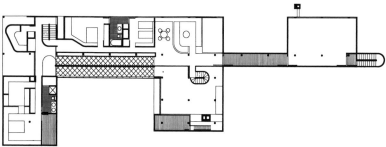

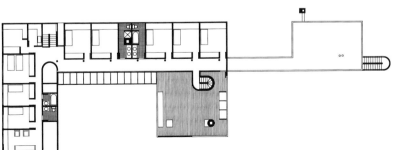

1970–1977 › Bronx Developmental Center
New York, New York, USA

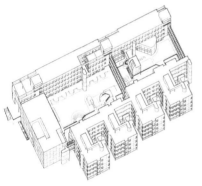

Commissioned by the Facilities Development Corporation for the New York State Department of Mental Hygiene, this building shows a closed façade to the relatively hostile, industrial environment.

As might be expected of Richard Meier, there are generous openings, but the location requires that they look inward rather than out. It is located on a triangular site with the Hutchinson River Parkway on one side, and railway tracks on another. Originally planned as a residential unit for 750 mentally or physically handicapped children, the completed facility is roughly half that size and accommodates 380 residents. The Center also cares for out-patients.

As described by the architect, "The two major programmatic elements divide around the lateral axis of the composition: the support services wing in the rectangular block on the west, and the residential units and services in the stepped volumes on the east. The gymnasium and physical therapy building on the south, and the two large courtyards, each with a corridor at its northern edge, stitch the composition together." A reflective natural aluminum finish on the building's metal panels differs from Richard Meier's more typical white surfaces, emphasizing an almost machine-like quality in the architecture.

1971–1973 · Douglas House
Harbor Springs, Michigan, USA

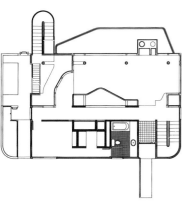

Surely one of the most frequently published of Richard Meier's early works, the Douglas House is set on a steeply sloped and forested site above Lake Michigan. Its distinct appearance against the wooded background, that of a "machined object perched in a natural world," explains some of its popularity for magazines, but it also highlights what might be called a utopian tendency in the architect's work. This perfect white object contrasts with its darker natural background, but the views it offers and the light it admits make it one with its surroundings. It is also one of the first of his buildings to bear such a close resemblance to a ship, with its nautical railings, sweeping decks, and projecting smokestacks.

Because of the slope, the residence is entered from the roof level at the rear via a bridge. The closed, east side facing a road predictably houses the private areas of the house. An entry vestibule immediately offers views into the public (dining and living) spaces and out to a roof deck, that dominates the lake. A skylight runs the length of this roof deck bringing sun into the living room below. With its three glazed walls, the living room is an essential space of the house where communion with the great lake in all seasons reaches its apogee. The penetration of nature into the house in the form of light and views to the outside is paralleled in the "unimpeded flow of space from inside to out," which may have a relation to Japanese architectural concepts.

1975–1979 · The Atheneum
New Harmony, Indiana, USA

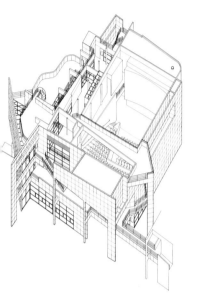

An isolated white beacon set near the Wabash River, this symbolic building is the starting point for the tour of a historic town founded in 1815 by the Harmony Society. With the arrival of Robert Owen in 1825, it came to be one of the best-known utopian communities in the United States.

This structure also bears comparison to Le Corbusier's Villa Savoye. There, too, an elevated mass is served by ramps with nautical railings. In this instance, visitors arrive by boat and are greeted on the flood plain of the river, justifying any reference to floating on the site. The spatial concept of the building imagines a continuous movement through the space, with the ramp as "chief mediator and armature." Two grids, with a five-degree shift between them, mark the plan, a frequent characteristic of Richard Meier's buildings, like the recurring ship metaphor. A steel-frame building clad with square porcelain-enameled panels, the Atheneum offers a light-filled space with numerous views of the surrounding countryside. Although the basic geometry of the plan is not overly complex, the rotation of its elements gives something akin to a sense of movement to the whole. Meier's description has it that, "As the ramp winds upward from the orthogonal grid and regains the five-degree offset orientation of the path from the river, the entire building is set in motion; the geometry of overlaid grids inducing a sense of spatial compression at certain points, tension at others, with grids almost colliding. This collision resonates throughout the complex interior as the ramp, illuminated by light from above, resolves the two grids in plan and section." An exhibition space on the third level is the ultimate destination of the visit and framed views of the town suggest what is to come for the tourists.

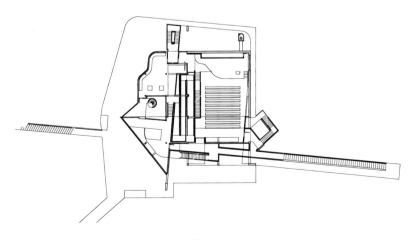

1978–2007 ▸ Arp Museum

Remagen-Rolandseck, Germany

Hans Arp (1886–1966) was a German-French sculptor, painter, and poet. He was one of the founding members of the Dada movement in Zurich in 1916. He married Sophie Taeuber-Arp, an equally well-known, Swiss artist in 1922.

Rolandseck is in the Rhineland-Palatinate region of Germany and is located close to Bonn. The site of the new museum is set on a wooded escarpment above the Rhine. Access to the Museum is through the "Künstler-Bahnhof," the former railway station of the town. A three-story entrance lobby contains the museum shop. A subterranean passage, including exhibition space, leads to an elevator that takes visitors up 131 feet (40 meters) to the new building. The Arp Museum displays a collection of works by Hans Arp and Sophie Taeuber-Arp and their circle, including sculpture, drawings, paintings, and textiles. Covering three levels and a total of 37 000 square feet (3 400 square meters), it includes an outdoor terrace on the northern side with a sculpture garden. The upper gallery is designed to let in overhead light.

Typically, "Clad in white enamel metal panels, the building is divided into a set of layered planes facing east, punctuated by glazed and louvered openings and cantilevered balconies affording panoramic views over the Rhine Valley."

1979–1985 ▸ Museum for the Decorative Arts
Frankfurt, Germany

In many respects, this is one of Richard Meier's most important buildings of the 1980s. Situated on the Museumsufer, on the opposite side of the Main from the downtown area of Frankfurt, and near other cultural institutions, the Museum for the Decorative Arts represents a first for the architect in that the plan integrates an existing 19th-century house, the Villa Metzler. Emphatically urban and public, it embodies a certain rejection of the Modernist isolation of the building as a free-standing object.

Meier introduced a 3.5° rotation of two overlaid grids, corresponding to the difference between the alignment of the Villa, which itself forms a near perfect cube (57.7 feet

[17.6 meters]), and the embankment of the Main. The fact that the architect uses this system of double grids throughout the design ties the Museum intimately to its site, even without respect to the precise built forms involved. The dimensions of each quadrant of the project are based on the size of the Villa. Meier's white, elsewhere associated with his Modernist inspiration, here recalls aspects of German Baroque architecture, or even, as he has said, examples of the German porcelain exhibited within.

"The project allowed me to make a work of art that forms a meaningful continuity with a broken cultural heritage," says Meier. The heritage he refers to here is undoubtedly that of his own family and others who left Germany in the turmoil leading up to World War II. As is the case in Atlanta, the free movement of visitors within the interior space allows the objects on display to be seen from various points of view, whether from a distance or at close proximity.

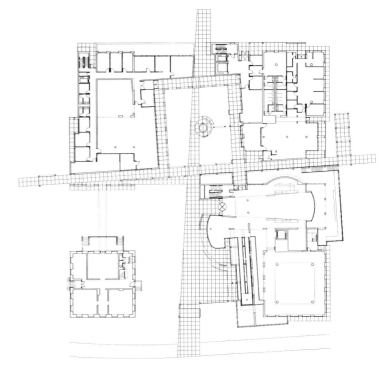

1980–1983 ▸ High Museum of Art

Atlanta, Georgia, USA

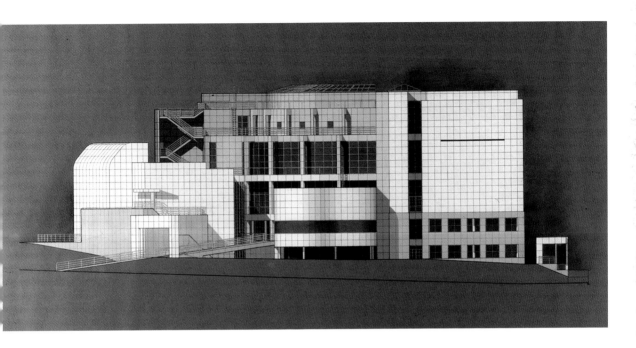

Set at the corner of Peachtree and Sixteenth Streets, roughly two miles (three kilometers) from downtown Atlanta, the High Museum was designed in four quadrants, with one being filled by a monumental entrance sequence and a four-story atrium. Richard Meier has indicated clearly that this central atrium was inspired by the design of Frank Lloyd Wright's Guggenheim in Manhattan. He has taken the opportunity, though, implicitly to criticize the older master in that the atrium is not intended to be used for the display of art, but rather as a gathering place for the residents of Atlanta. The fact that art is not displayed in this space also allowed the architect to freely place windows offering views of the city.

The High Museum shares the concept of a long entry ramp with the Atheneum, but the structure in Georgia appears to be much more inward looking than the one in Indiana. Though the ramp does represent a clear invitation to enter, the life of this building is located within. The High Museum includes about 54 000 square feet (5 000 square meters) of exhibition space for works that can be viewed from many different angles as visitors progress through the space of the building. A 200-seat auditorium is also part of the facility. As is so often the case in Richard Meier's architecture, his preoccupation with light, which informs and indeed shapes the space, is amply in evidence here.

Due to the increasing size of the city and the success of Meier's design, the High Museum has seen a constant increase in its visitor numbers. This led the institution to call on the architect Renzo Piano to create three new buildings in 2005, doubling the size of the overall facility to almost 312 000 square feet (29 000 square meters).

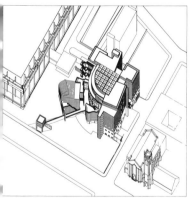

1984–1989 · Grotta House
Harding Township, New Jersey, USA

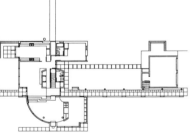

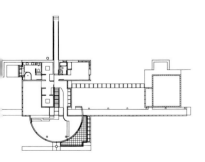

Gray enamel paneling is an unexpected feature of the Grotta House, which may come as close to the kind of perfection Richard Meier has sought as any of his buildings. This is in part due to the client, a childhood friend of Meier's with a vision of his house that allows for no stray objects. Mr. Grotta found space only for the architecture, necessary furniture, and his own collection of pottery and popular art. Though an almost fanatical admirer of Richard Meier's architecture, Grotta also interviewed the Canadian architect Arthur Erikson, before settling on his friend.

Set on a beautiful 7-acre (2.5-hectare) sloping meadowland site in a rural area of New Jersey, the main internal space of the house is structured around a central cylindrical double-height (22-foot- [6.7-meter-] high) living room. Like a reminder of earlier Meier houses, a bridge enters the house from the rear, where the original design called for a swimming pool. A covered walkway connects the house to a parking area, and serves as the main entrance. Aside from the gray paneling, another unusual surface feature of the Grotta House is the use of a ground-faced concrete block at the back and kitchen side of the house. The meadow site of this house makes the contrast of its geometric forms all the more obvious.

By using simple forms at the base of the design, the architect rotates, bisects, and elaborates them until a musical complexity arises and is brought to life by his masterly use of natural light.

1984–1997 · The Getty Center
Los Angeles, California, USA

In many respects, this is the most prestigious commission accorded to an American architect in the final quarter of the 20th century. Set on a spectacular 110-acre (44.5-hectare) hilltop site near the Brentwood area of Los Angeles, it is a 947 000-square-foot (88 000-square-meter) six-building complex that groups together the activities of the Getty Trust, including a museum. Richard Meier himself has compared the Center to an Italian hilltop town, and the use of a rugged cleft travertine for much of the cladding does give the whole a much warmer or more Mediterranean feel than the pure white buildings for which Meier is best known. The Mediterranean image is also appropriate to the circulation established between the buildings—flowered courtyards and open walkways give the whole a congenial atmosphere, which is different from the rather mathematical precision that often characterizes Meier's work. This is also due to the southern California climate that favors vegetation, and offers ample, warm sunlight. An unexpected note is added in the Museum interiors, where Thierry Despont was responsible for giving a markedly traditional air to the galleries.

"In my mind's eye I see a classic structure, elegant and timeless, emerging, serene and ideal, from the rough hillside, a kind of Aristotelian structure within the landscape,"

said Richard Meier some years ago. It is indeed this classical image that prevails in the Getty Center, despite the marked modernity of Meier's plans. This group of buildings seems to have been conceived by client and architect alike with posterity in mind. The very solidity of the Getty Center is somehow removed from the ephemeral architecture of most of Los Angeles, as is the decidedly European tone of the collections and the globe-straddling nature of the Center's activities.

The Getty Center may be too complex in its layout for the taste of some, too much an exercise in architectural virtuosity for others. It is hard to classify this as a purely Modernist design despite the overall reliance on geometric forms. The Getty Center is in a class apart, because of its billion-dollar budget, but also because of its cultural functions, the ambitions of its directors, and the ways in which the architect has risen to a once-in-a-lifetime challenge.

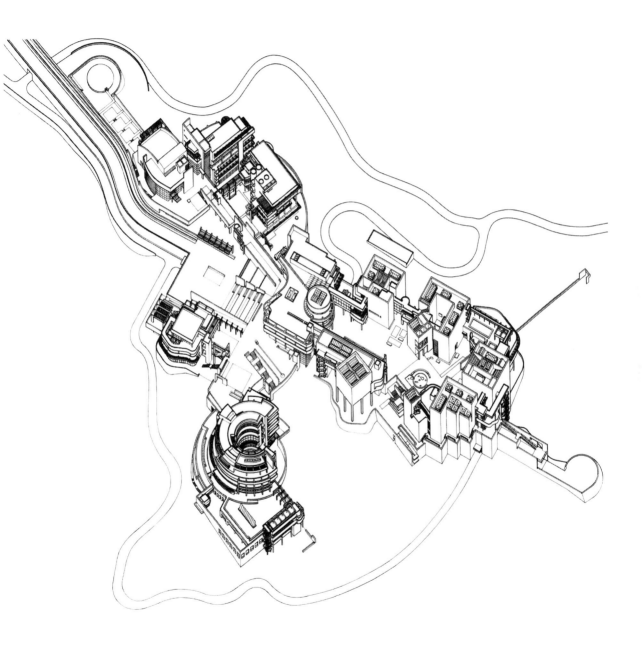

1986–1993 ▸ Stadthaus
Ulm, Germany

The Stadthaus civic center in Ulm was dedicated on November 12, 1993. The 38 000-square-foot (3 500-square-meter) three-story complex clad in Rosa Dante granite and white stucco, without any metal panels, houses exhibition spaces, a large assembly hall, a café, and a tourist information center.

It is notable not only for its own design, but also for the ways in which Richard Meier has resolved the complex problems posed by the site on Münsterplatz, which he was also called upon to repave.

The 528-foot- (161-meter-) tall Ulm Münster, a Lutheran cathedral, dominates the historic center of this town of 120 000. Bombing in 1944 destroyed 85% of the Old Town, and the reconstruction of Ulm was carried out without much regard for the quality of the architecture. Aside from having the tallest cathedral spire in the world, Ulm is known as the birthplace of Albert Einstein. The curving, pedestrian Bahnhofstrasse leads from

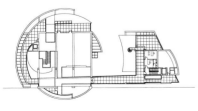

the train station to the square, where Meier has placed a curved wall that leads people into the square. A glass bridge with a pedestrian underpass links the two basic elements of the structure, facilitating movement through the space, as do the numerous possible points of entry.

As Meier points out, one of the interesting features of the building is the proliferation of views of the Münster spire throughout the building. "Following more than a century of unsuccessful attempts at invigorating this cathedral square," he says, "the new exhibit and assembly building has demonstrated how design and building expertise, focused on one site-specific work, can completely metamorphose the city and mediate modern form with historic context."

1987–1995·Museum of Contemporary Art
Barcelona, Spain

Located in the area of the Casa de la Caritat, a former monastic enclave in the Old City of Barcelona, this building includes a ramp leading to the main entry and to a three-story cylindrical reception area, with an opening into the large, flexible galleries. The design takes up a number of the site's existing paths and routes, making it fit into the old, dark neighborhood far more than it might have, had the design been purely Modernist in the most rigorous sense. A public sculpture garden and a plaza in front of the Museum are part of the scheme.

As Richard Meier tells the story, "At dinner one night in New York a number of years ago I met Mayor Pasqual Maragall of Barcelona, who was the guest of honor. He asked me what type of building I would like to do in Barcelona. My answer was simple, a museum."

The main entry raised above the plaza, on the south façade is framed by an overhanging screen and is reached via a ramp. The lobby of the structure is cylindrical and a ramp rises through the triple-height glazed atrium. Translucent glass-block floors "create a welcoming light-saturated environment." An enameled panel wall runs through the building's spine and the actual galleries are conceived as "loft-like spaces" of various dimensions, in an effort to accommodate the often unexpected demands of contemporary art. By way of contrast with the dark façades and labyrinthine street plan of the Barri Gótic district in which it is located, the Museum stands out like a utopian dream, rational and white, and yet it is intimately related to its site. As he did in Ulm in a less dense urban setting, Richard Meier has proven in Barcelona that he is amply capable of dealing with the demands of the historic cities of Europe.

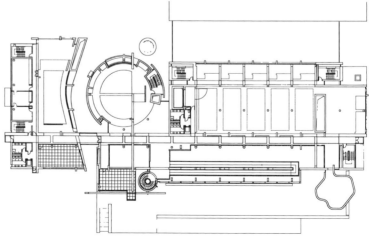

1988–1992▸Canal+ Headquarters
Paris, France

"I like to think of this building as Parisian in feeling," says Richard Meier, "intellectual yet sensual, and beautiful in its rationality. Spatially it is simple, but technically it is complex. The building's sheer wall becomes the placard both for Canal+ and its urban presence. Its image from the Seine is of a great ship whose only movement is the changing light."

The headquarters for one of the most successful cable television companies in France, this building is located in the 15th arrondissement, adjoining the André Citroën Park and close to the Pont Mirabeau. Built on a very tight schedule between April 1990 and the end of 1991, the building has 237 000 square feet (22 000 square meters) of usable space. Three four-story television studios that Richard Meier was not called on to design determined the form of the block on the eastern side, and there were severe zoning restrictions, such as differing height requirements, while the L-shaped site itself posed problems. The western administration wing faces the Seine.

Light is omnipresent in this inspiring structure. With the large parabolic antennas on its roof, the Canal+ building projects just the sort of forward-looking image that the former director of the firm, André Rousselet, wanted when he called on Richard Meier. As the architect's description has it, "Conceptually, Canal+ depends on a series of delicately tessellated membranes. Of primary importance is the combination of clear, translucent, and opaque white glass that makes up the curtain wall on the river façade, in conjunction with the projecting, lightweight aluminum *brise-soleils* along its entire length. A similar curtain wall is on the southern façade of the audiovisual wing facing the park. The aerodynamic thrust of the office wing-wall opening to the river, and the broad, contrasting mass of the studios bring new life and a sense of civic destiny to this neighborhood."

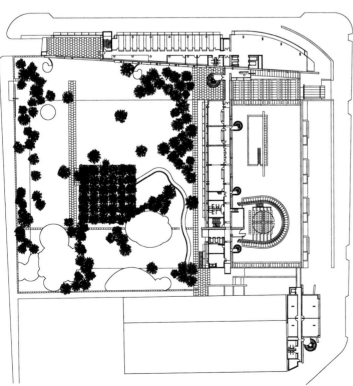

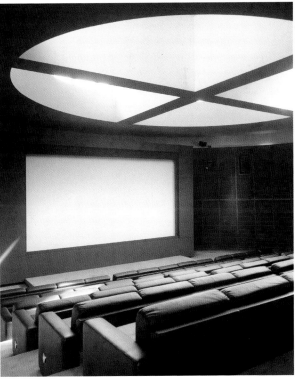

1995–1998▸Neugebauer House

Naples, Florida, USA

Located in the southwestern Florida community of Naples, on the Bay of Doubloon, this house has an unusual 'V'-shaped roof. The architect explains that local regulations required a slanted roof, but did not indicate the direction of the slant. Using 1.2-inch- (3-centimeter-) thick glass for heat insulation, he also devised a complex system of *brise-soleils*.

As is usually the case of Meier, public and private areas of the Neugebauer House are clearly divided. The horizontal, shed-like design of the house, however, represents a change in the architect's options. Here he has chosen more complex, articulated geometric forms than in many of his other houses, as is also the case in another of his waterfront homes, the Ackerberg House in California. He of course retains his preference for a white, light-filled architecture. The architect's explanation of the disposition of the interior spaces is clear and instructive: "The house's linear organization consists of four parallel layers which are organized from front to back. A raised, main entry penetrates a wall of limestone which protects the front layer: a skylit corridor which runs the entire length of the house. A 12-foot- (3.66-meter-) wide bar/module strictly orders the dimensions of all open, communal and closed, cellular spaces. The primary spaces, including bedrooms and living spaces, are arranged in linear formation, providing each room with an impressive view over the lap pool to the Bay beyond."

Meier's surprising use of an inverted sloped roof shows his capacity to innovate within the confines of his own strict vocabulary, and this house remains one of his most powerful.

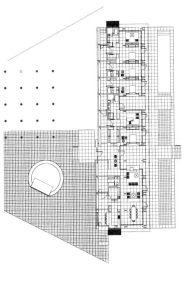

1996–2003 · Jubilee Church
Rome, Italy

The Jubilee Church (Dio Padre Misericordioso, Tor Tre Teste) is located on a triangular site outside central Rome and is designed around three shells or arcs that evoke billowing white sails. The architect has also elected to divide the structure into distinct precincts, with the sacred realm to the south (nave), and the secular space to the north. A community center is part of the complex, and both the church and the center can be reached from the east via a paved entrance plaza. Despite its apparently unorthodox sail design, the proportions of the structure are based on a series of displaced squares and four circles. As Meier says, "Three circles of equal radius generate the profiles of the three shells that, together with the spine-wall, make up the body of the nave. While the three shells discreetly imply the Holy Trinity, the reflecting pool symbolizes water in the ritual of Baptism." Natural light is of course important both in viewing the exterior volumes and within the church itself.

Winner of a competition in which Tadao Ando, Günter Behnisch, Santiago Calatrava, Peter Eisenman, and Frank Gehry also participated, in the spring of 1996, Meier as usual placed an emphasis on white forms and natural light. "Light is the protagonist of our understanding and reading of space. Light is the means by which we are able to experience what we call sacred. Light is at the origin of this building."

Inaugurated on October 26, 2003, to mark the 25th anniversary of the Pontificate of John Paul II, Dio Padre Misericordioso was Meier's first church, although he had previously designed a chapel.

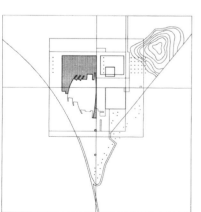

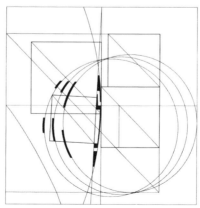

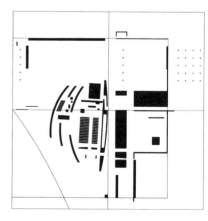

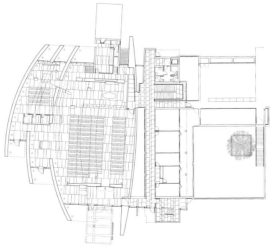

1996–2006▸Ara Pacis Museum
Rome, Italy

The Ara Pacis Augustae (meaning "Altar of Majestic Peace") is an altar to peace, envisioned as a Roman goddess. It was commissioned by Emperor Augustus, and consecrated on January 30, 9 BC, by the Senate to celebrate the peace established in the Empire after Augustus's victories in Gaul and Spain. Located on the Campus Martius near the Tiber, it was buried under silt and rediscovered in the 16th century.

In 1938, Mussolini had a protective structure designed by Vittorio Ballio Morpurgo on the Piazza Augusto Imperatore, near the mausoleum of Augustus. As the first work of modern architecture built in the historic center of Rome since the 1930s, Richard Meier's new protective structure was the object of a great deal of anticipation and controversy.

A glass curtain wall 44 feet (13.5 meters) high and 164 feet (50 meters) long floods the interior with light. Seven, thin, reinforced-concrete columns mark the darker 28-foot-(8.5-meter-) high entry hall that leads to the altar itself. A low wall clad in beige Roman travertine marble marks the original shoreline of the Tiber near the structure. The building includes 7500 square feet (700 square meters) of exhibition space, a digital library, outdoor roof terrace, auditorium, bar, and café.

Working in the difficult political context of Rome and with a mixture of ancient and Fascist architecture (Piazza Augusto Imperatore), Meier has faced one of the most precarious balancing acts of his career with the Ara Pacis Museum.

1998–2005 ‧ San Jose City Hall

San Jose, California, USA

Part of a seven-block redevelopment area in downtown San Jose, the new Civic Center is to be accompanied by a future theater and concert hall. The large (540000-square-foot [50000-square-meter]) complex includes an 18-story tower and two lower structures intended to house city departments and meeting rooms. The construction budget for the project was $192 million. Ample light and ventilation are provided, with an emphasis on energy-efficient, sustainable systems. A landscaped grove in the public outdoor plaza recalls the significance of agriculture for the local economy.

The main entrance to the complex brings visitors through this plaza. Up to 2000 persons can gather in the outdoor area. The partially glazed and louvered entrance rotunda rises eight stories, and a ceremonial staircase rises from there to the second-floor city-council chambers. The tower rises behind the dome and is "subtly layered and orchestrated to create an elaborately sun-screened low relief." While making reference to typical themes in civic architecture (the dome), Meier succeeds in creating a bright modernity that has nothing to do with the heavy symbolism of the past, as is indeed appropriate for the California community.

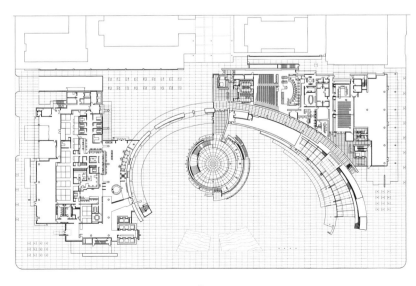

1999–2001 ▸ Southern California Beach House

Malibu, Southern California, USA

The Pacific Coast Highway runs from Dana Point to Oxnard in southern California. Notable sections such as that running past Santa Monica are lined on the oceanside with remarkable residences. Meier's own Ackerberg House is near the Pacific Coast Highway in Malibu. This Beach House is located directly on the beach with magnificent open vistas of the Pacific Ocean. A glazed, translucent entry in the center of the house on the roadside reveals a grass courtyard and a single tree planted within the perimeter of the residence. The two-story entrance hall immediately offers visitors the view of the water. A double-height glazed living room prolonged by a wooden deck look out onto the beach. Sliding glass doors create a tangible continuity between exterior and interior.

Although the climate of southern California does not really recall that of Japan, the fundamental ambiguity between inside and outside is very much a part of Japanese architectural tradition. As the architect explains the structure, "The beams at the roof level, located above the fenestration, express the structural rhythm and layering of the components. This cadence is echoed in the pattern of the painted aluminum wall panels and modular windows. Elsewhere, the external plaster walls are juxtaposed with the transparent glazed façades, creating a mosaic of layered materials. This use of layered wall elements, intersected by transparent surfaces, dissolves the separation between inside and outside throughout the house."

84

1999–2002 · 173/176 Perry Street

New York, New York, USA

Few buildings have had as strong an impact on residential construction in Manhattan as Richard Meier's two towers at 173/176 Perry Street, in Greenwich Village. Whereas promoters were often somewhat dubious about the advantages of pairing with famous designers, the success of Meier's Perry Street project has been at the origin of a series of other condominium schemes in Manhattan, all involving well-known architects.

Both 15 stories tall, the buildings look out onto the Hudson River and the New Jersey shore opposite, and mark the first time Meier erected a building in the city where he lives and works. The architectural concrete cores of the buildings are located to the rear (east) in order to maximize the views through the floor-to-ceiling curtain-glass walls at the front of the building. Clad in insulating laminated glass and white metal panels, the structures stand out from their more traditional environment. The tower at 176 Perry Street has a larger footprint and contains one apartment on each floor with a gross area of 3750 square feet (348 square meters). Adding to the allure of the apartments, often acquired by well-known personalities, the larger building houses star chef Jean-Georges Vongerichten's Perry Street restaurant. The small tower, at 173 Perry Street, has apartments with a floor area of 1817 square feet (169 square meters).

The buildings take advantage of the recently renovated Hudson River Park that runs along the river from lower Manhattan to 59th Street. Richard Meier completed his third building in the neighborhood at 165 Charles Street in 2006.

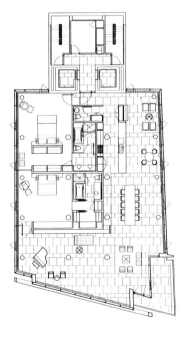

2003–2006 ▸ 165 Charles Street

New York, New York, USA

Parallel to Perry Street, Charles Street is very close to the site of Richard Meier's earlier condominium towers. The 16-story building is 180 feet (55 meters) high and includes 31 apartments for a total of 100 000 square feet (9 290 square meters). Conceived to "continue the urban form and crystalline character of the Perry Street apartments," most of the building is designed to house a pair of two-bedroom apartments on each floor. Whereas the Perry Street apartments were created as open-ended loft spaces, the Charles Street apartments were planned by Meier down to the last detail. The second floor of the tower includes four one-bedroom apartments with double-height living/dining rooms. A penthouse occupies the uppermost level of the building. As the architect explains, "Apart from the common crystalline syntax, the elevations of this residential block differ significantly from the plastic character of the Perry Street development, above all in the absence of inset balconies and in the surface treatment of the elevator/stair tower. The relative narrowness of the Charles Street site dictates a more contained approach."

The three towers are visible as a continuous development and immediately give the impression of being variations on a theme, with the Charles Street building being even more visibly glazed and open than its predecessors.

Although other architects have left a significant mark on the architecture of Manhattan, Meier's grouping of these three towers in a relatively short span of time and space gives them an arresting urban quality—a call to improve the architecture of the city that clearly is being heard.

Life and Work

1934 ▸ *Richard Meier is born in Newark, New Jersey*

1952–57 ▸ *He receives his architectural training at Cornell University*

1960 ▸ *He works for Skidmore, Owings & Merrill, New York*

1961–63 ▸ *He works for Marcel Breuer, New York*

1962
Lambert House, Fire Island, New York

1963 ▸ *Richard Meier establishes his own practice in New York.*
Recent American Synagogue Architecture, The Jewish Museum, New York, New York
House for Carolyn and Jerome Meier, Essex Fells, New Jersey (–1965)

1964
Monumental Fountain, competition entry (with Frank Stella), Philadelphia, Pennsylvania
Sona Store (with Elaine Lustig Cohen), New York, New York
Dotson House, Ithaca, New York (–1966, unbuilt)
Renfeld House (with Elaine Lustig Cohen), Chester, New Jersey (–1966)

1965
Stella Studio and Apartment, New York, New York
University Arts Center, competition entry (with John Hejduk and Robert Slutzky), Berkeley, California (unbuilt)
Smith House, Darien, Connecticut (–1967)

1966
Mental Health Facilities, West Orange, New Jersey (unbuilt)
Rubin Loft Renovation, New York, New York
Hoboken Center Waterfront Renewal Project (with John Hejduk and Robert Slutzky), Hoboken, New Jersey (unbuilt)
Hoffman House, East Hampton, New York (–1967)

1967
Saltzman House, East Hampton, New York (–1969)
Westbeth Artists' Housing, New York, New York (–1970)

1968
Fredonia Health and Physical Education Building, Fredonia, New York (unbuilt)

1969
Charles Evans Industrial Buildings, Fairfield and Piscataway, New Jersey (unbuilt)
Bronx Redevelopment Planning Study, New York, New York
House in Pound Ridge, Pound Ridge, New York (unbuilt)
Old Westbury House, Old Westbury, New York (–1971)
Monroe Developmental Center (with Todd & Giroux, Architects), Rochester, New York (–1974)
Twin Parks Northeast Housing, New York, New York (–1974)

1970
Bronx Developmental Center, New York, New York (–1977)

1971
Branch Office Prototype for Olivetti, six locations in the U.S. (unbuilt)
Modification of the Olivetti Branch Office Prototype, seven locations in the U.S. (unbuilt)
Dormitory for the Olivetti Training Center, Tarrytown, New York (unbuilt)
Olivetti Headquarters Building, Fairfax, Virginia (unbuilt)
Douglas House, Harbor Springs, Michigan (–1973)
Maidman House, Sands Point, New York (–1976)

1972
East Side Housing (with Emery Roth, Architects), New York, New York
Shamberg House, Chappaqua, New York (–1974)

1973
Museum of Modern Art at the Villa Strozzi, Florence, Italy (unbuilt)

Right:
Richard Meier with his daughter Ana

1974
Condominium Housing, Yonkers, New York
(unbuilt)
Cornell University Undergraduate Housing,
Ithaca, New York (unbuilt)

1975
Commercial Building and Hotel, Springfield,
Massachusetts (unbuilt)
Warehouse Rehabilitation for the Bronx
Psychiatric Center, New York, New York (−1978)
Sarah Campbell Blaffer Pottery Studio, New
Harmony, Indiana (−1978)
The Atheneum, New Harmony, Indiana (−1979)

1976
Suburban House Prototype, Concord,
Massachusetts
Opening Exhibition, Cooper-Hewitt Museum,
New York, New York

1977
Manchester Civic Center, Manchester, New
Hampshire (unbuilt)
New York School Exhibition, State Museum,
Albany, New York
Aye Simon Reading Room, Solomon R. Guggen-
heim Museum, New York, New York (−1978)
Apartment for Mr. and Mrs. Philip Suarez, New
York, New York (−1978)
Palm Beach House, Palm Beach, Florida (−1979,
unbuilt)

1978
Hartford Seminary, Hartford, Connecticut (−1981)
Clifty Creek Elementary School, Columbus,
Indiana (−1982)
Furniture for Knoll International (−1982)
Arp Museum, Remagen-Rolandseck, Germany
(−2007)

1979
Irwin Union Bank and Trust Company, Columbus,
Indiana (unbuilt)
Giovannitti House, Pittsburgh, Pennsylvania
(−1983)
Museum for the Decorative Arts, Frankfurt,
Germany (−1985)

1980
Somerset Condominiums, Beverly Hills, California
(unbuilt)
East 67th Street Housing, New York, New York
(unbuilt)
Objects for Alessi Designs
Meier/Stella Collaboration (with Frank Stella)
High Museum of Art, Atlanta, Georgia (−1983)

1981
Renault Administrative Headquarters, Boulogne-
Billancourt, France (unbuilt)

1982
Internationale Bauausstellung Housing, Berlin,
Germany (unbuilt)
Parc de la Villette, competition entry, Paris, France
(unbuilt)
Des Moines Art Center Addition, Des Moines,
Iowa (−1984)

1983
Opéra Bastille, competition entry, Paris, France
(unbuilt)
Lingotto Factory Conversion, Turin, Italy (unbuilt)
Tableware for Swid-Powell Designs (−1984)
Office Building for Siemens, Munich, Germany
(−1999)

1984 ▸ *Richard Meier becomes the youngest
winner to receive the Pritzker Prize*
Helmick House, Des Moines, Iowa (unbuilt)
Westchester House, Westchester County, New
York (−1986)
Ackerberg House, Malibu, California (−1986)

Bridgeport Center, Bridgeport, Connecticut
(−1989)
Barnum Museum, Bridgeport, Connecticut (−1989,
unbuilt)
Grotta House, Harding Township, New Jersey
(−1989)
The Getty Center, Los Angeles, California (−1997)

1985
Siemens Office and Laboratory Complex, Munich,
Germany (−1989)

1986
Offices, Richard Meier & Partners, New York and
Los Angeles
Supreme Court Building, competition entry,
Jerusalem, Israel (unbuilt)
Progetto Bicocca, competition entry, Milan, Italy
(unbuilt)
Progetto per Napoli, Naples, Italy (unbuilt)
Stadthaus, Ulm, Germany (−1993)
City Hall and Central Library, The Hague, The
Netherlands (−1995)

1987
Eye Center (in association with GBD Architects),
Portland, Oregon (unbuilt)
National Investment Bank, The Hague, The
Netherlands (unbuilt)
Santa Monica Beach Hotel, competition entry,
Santa Monica, California (unbuilt)
Madison Square Garden Site Redevelopment,
competition entry, New York, New York (unbuilt)
Weishaupt Forum, Schwendi, Germany (−1992)
Royal Dutch Paper Mills Headquarters,
Hilversum, The Netherlands (−1992)
Museum of Contemporary Art, Barcelona, Spain
(−1995)

1988
Cornell University Alumni and Admissions Center,
Ithaca, New York (unbuilt)
Canal+ Headquarters, Paris, France (−1992)
Espace Pitôt, Montpellier, France (−1995)

1989 ▸ *Richard Meier receives the RIBA (Royal
Institute of British Architects) Gold Medal*
Administrative and Maritime Center Master Plan,
Antwerp, Belgium

bliothèque de France, competition entry, Paris,
rance (unbuilt)
uandt Office Building, Frankfurt, Germany
nbuilt)
dinburgh Park Master Plan, Edinburgh, Scotland
aimler-Benz Research Center, Ulm, Germany
-1992)
ypolux Bank Building, Luxembourg (−1993)
useum of Ethnology, Frankfurt, Germany (−1996,
nbuilt)

990

ox Studios Expansion and Renovation, Los
ngeles, California (unbuilt)
extius-Mirabeau Master Plan, competition entry,
ix-en-Provence, France (unbuilt)
uregio Office Building, Basel, Switzerland (−1998)
amden Medical Center, Singapore (−1999)

991

Office Building, Berlin, Germany (unbuilt)
abric Designs for DesignTex
ight Fixtures for Baldinger
lateau Tercier Master Plan, Nice, France
wissair North American Headquarters, Melville,
New York (−1995)
achofsky House, Dallas, Texas (−1996)

992

otsdamer Platz Master Plan, competition entry,
erlin, Germany (unbuilt)
Office Furniture for Stow Davis

993

dministrative Building, Marckolsheim, France
unbuilt)
Ackerberg House Addition, Malibu, California
−1995)
Alfonse M. D'Amato United States Courthouse,
slip, New York (−2000)

994

Berliner Volksbank Headquarters, competition
entry, Berlin, Germany (unbuilt)
Compaq Computer Administrative, Manufacturing
and Distribution Center Master Plan, Houston,
Texas (unbuilt)
Gagosian Gallery, Beverly Hills, California (−1995)
Museum of Television and Radio, Beverly Hills,

California (−1996)
Sandra Day O'Connor United States Courthouse,
Phoenix, Arizona (−2000)

1995

Swiss Re Headquarters, competition entry,
Kingston, New York (unbuilt)
Grand Piano for Rud. Ibach Sohn
Neugebauer House, Naples, Florida (−1998)

1996

Coordinated Street Furniture, New York, New York
Kolonihavehus, Copenhagen, Denmark (unbuilt)
Cittadella Bridge, Alessandria, Italy (unbuilt)
Jubilee Church, Rome, Italy (−2003)
Ara Pacis Museum, Rome, Italy (−2006)

1997 ▶ *Richard Meier receives the AIA Gold
Medal, the highest award from the American
Institute of Architects, and, in the same year, the
Praemium Imperiale from the Japanese
government in recognition of a lifetime
achievement in the arts*
Glasgow Exhibition House, Glasgow, Scotland
Tag McLaren Headquarters, Surrey, England
(unbuilt)
Indoor/Outdoor Seating for MABEG Kreuschner
Westwood Promenade, Los Angeles, California
(−1998)
Kuala Lumpur House, Kuala Lumpur, Malaysia
(−2003)

1998

Deutsche Post Building, competition entry, Bonn,
Germany (unbuilt)

Headquarters for Bayer AG, competition entry,
Leverkusen, Germany (unbuilt)
Scottish Parliament, competition entry,
Edinburgh, Scotland (unbuilt)
Friesen House, Los Angeles, California (−2000)
Peek & Cloppenburg Department Store,
Düsseldorf, Germany (−2001)
Rickmers Headquarters, Hamburg, Germany
(−2001)
Canon Headquarters, Tokyo, Japan (−2002)
International Center for Possibility Thinking,
Garden Grove, California (−2003)
San Jose City Hall, San Jose, California (−2005)

1999

Frankfurt Forum, competition entry, Frankfurt,
Germany (unbuilt)
Chesterfield Village, Chesterfield, Missouri
(unbuilt)
Swartz House, Laguna Beach, California (unbuilt)
Trinity College, competition entry, Dublin, Ireland
(unbuilt)
Canary Wharf, competition entry, London,
England (unbuilt)
Swartz House, Laguna Beach, California (−2000)
Southern California Beach House, Malibu,
Southern California (−2001)
173/176 Perry Street, New York, New York (−2002)
Santa Ynez House, Santa Ynez, California (−2002)
Painted Turtle Camp, Lake Hughes, California
(−2003)
UCLA Broad Art Center, Los Angeles, California
(−2006)
Hotel Raphael renovations, Rome, Italy (−2007)
Scenario Lane, Los Angeles, California (−2007)

2000

Arabia Product Design
Robert Bosch Foundation Buildings, competition entry, Stuttgart, Germany (unbuilt)
Country House, New York State (unbuilt)
Düsseldorf Harbor, Düsseldorf, Germany (unbuilt)
Draycott Park, Singapore (–2001, unbuilt)
Pankrác City Master Plan, Prague, Czech Republic (–2010)

2001

Performing Arts Center, Bethel, New York (unbuilt)
Yale University History of Art and Arts Library Building, New Haven, Connecticut (unbuilt)
Santa Barbara House, Santa Barbara, California
Habsburgerring Tower, Cologne, Germany (unbuilt)
Wijnhaven Quarter Urban Development and Program Study, The Hague, The Netherlands (unbuilt)
Viking Research Center, Starkville, Mississippi (–2003)
Burda Collection Museum, Baden-Baden, Germany (–2004)
Joy Apartment, New York, New York (–2006)
Peek & Cloppenburg Department Store, Mannheim, Germany (–2007)
Weill Hall, Cornell University, Ithaca, New York (–2008)
ECM City Tower, Prague, Czech Republic (–2008)
University of Bologna Master Plan, Bologna, Italy (–2010)

2002

Gagosian Gallery Addition, Beverly Hills, California
House at Sagaponac, Long Island, New York
Grand Hotel Salone (with Poliform), Milan Furniture Fair, Milan, Italy
Avery Fisher Hall, Lincoln Center (competition entry with Arata Isozaki), New York, New York (unbuilt)
The Urban Facility-Downtown Manhattan Project for the *New York Times*, New York, New York
Greenpoint Landing Master Plan, Brooklyn, New York (unbuilt)
World Trade Center Memorial Square, New York, New York, (competition entry with Eisenman

Architects, Gwathmey Siegel & Associates, Steven Holl Architects) (unbuilt)
66 Restaurant, New York, New York (–2003)
Zaragoza House, Corona del Mar, California (–2003)
Spyglass Hill Residence, Newport Beach, California (–2004)
Feldmühleplatz Office Buildings, Düsseldorf, Germany (–2004)
Malibu Beach House, Malibu, California (–2006)
Hamburg America Center, Hamburg, Germany (–2008)

2003

Kojaian Apartment, New York, New York
165 Charles Street, New York, New York (–2006)
Millennium Plaza, Los Angeles, California (–2006)
Jesolo Lido Village, Jesolo, Italy (–2007)
Jesolo Lido Hotel and Condominium , Jesolo, Italy (–2008)
Prospect Park Condominium, Brooklyn, New York (–2008)
Rickmers House, Hamburg, Germany (–2008)
Saint-Denis Office Complex, Paris, France (–2008)
United States Courthouse, San Diego, California (–2010)

2004

Beach House Condominium, Miami, Florida (unbuilt)
Southern Florida House, Palm Beach, Florida (–2005)
CUT and sidebar by Wolfgang Puck, Beverly Hills, California (–2006)
Gans House, San Francisco, California (–2007)
Neumann Headquarters, Hamburg, Germany (–2009)
9900 Wilshire, Beverly Hills, California (–2010)
Mandeville Place, Philadelphia, Pennsylvania (–2010)
East River Master Plan, New York, New York (–2012)

2005

Playa Grande, Dominican Republic
Hotel in Las Vegas, Las Vegas, Nevada (unbuilt)
Project Sandbox, Malibu, California (–2006, unbuilt)
Houses in Shenzhen, Shenzhen, China (–2008)

Italcementi Center for Research and Innovation, Bergamo, Italy (–2009)

2006

Palace in Dubai, Dubai, United Arab Emirates (unbuilt)
MoMA West Tower, New York, New York (unbuilt)
Office Tower, Osaka, Japan (unbuilt)
Charles Street Penthouse, New York, New York (–2007)
Midtown Apartment, New York, New York (–2007)
Canyon View House, Los Angeles, California (–2007)
Albion Riverside Penthouse, London, England (–2008)
All Saints Church Addition, Pasadena, California (–2009)
California Beach House, Malibu, California (–2009)
La Raphaelina Hotel and Condominium, Rome, Italy (–2011)

2007

Mixed-Use Tower, Warsaw, Poland (unbuilt)
Newark Housing Typology Study, Newark, New Jersey
LTB Media Headquarters, New York, New York (–2008)
IMG World Headquarters, New York, New York (–2008)
Flying Point House, Southampton, New York (–2009)
Houses in Yalikavak, Yalikavak, Turkey (–2009)
Luxembourg House, Luxembourg (–2009)
Rothschild Tower, Tel Aviv, Israel (–2010)
Beverly Hills House, Beverly Hills, California (–2010)
Symphony in the Glen, Los Angeles, California (–2010)

2008 ▶ *Richard Meier is a member of the Board of Trustees of the Cooper-Hewitt Museum, the American Academy in Rome and the American Academy of Arts and Letters from which he received the Gold Medal for Architecture in 2008*

Map

Projects listed in this book:

France
Paris: Canal+ Headquartes

Germany
Frankfurt: Museum for the Decorative Arts

Remagen-Rolandseck: Arp Museum

Ulm: Stadthaus

Italy
Rome: Ara Pacis Museum, Jubilee Church

Spain
Barcelona: Museum of Contemporary Art

USA
Atlanta, Georgia: High Museum of Art

Darien, Connecticut: Smith House

East Hampton, New York: Saltzman House

Harbor Springs, Michigan: Douglas House

Harding Township, New Jersey: Grotta House

Los Angeles, California: The Getty Center

Malibu, Southern California: Southern California Beach House

Naples, Florida: Neugebauer House

New Harmony, Indiana: The Atheneum

New York, New York: Bronx Developmental Center, 165 Charles Street, 173/176 Perry Street

Old Westbury, New York: Old Westbury House

San Jose, California: San Jose City Hall

Bibliography

▶ Werner Blaser, *Richard Meier, Details*, Basel, Boston: Birkhauser, 1996

▶ Michael Brawne, *Richard Meier. Museum für Kunsthandwerk*, London: Phaidon Press, 1992

▶ Michael Brawne, *The Getty Center. Richard Meier & Partners, Architecture in Detail*, London: Phaidon Press, 1998

▶ Ingeborg Flagge, Oliver Hamm (eds.), *Richard Meier in Europe*, Berlin: Ernst & Sohn, 1997

▶ Lisa Green (ed.), *Richard Meier Architect. 1985/1991. Volume 2*, with essays by Joseph Rykwert and Kenneth Frampton, New York: Rizzoli, 1991

▶ Lisa Green (ed.), *Richard Meier. Architect. 1992/1999. Volume 3*, with essays by Joseph Rykwert and Kenneth Frampton, New York: Rizzoli, 1999

▶ Philip Jodidio, *Meier. Richard Meier & Partners. Complete Works 1963–2008*, Cologne: Taschen, 2008

▶ *Richard Meier Architect*, essays by Stan Allen (et al), New York: Monacelli, 1999

▶ Richard Meier, *Building the Getty*, Berkeley: University of California Press, 1999

▶ *Richard Meier Houses. 1962–1967*, essays by Paul Goldberger and Richard Rogers, New York: Rizzoli, 1996

▶ Joan Ockman (ed.), *Richard Meier. Architect. 1964/1984. Volume 1*, New York: Rizzoli, 1984

▶ Manfred Sack, *Richard Meier. Stadthaus Ulm*, Stuttgart: Edition Axel Menges, 1995

▶ Elizabeth White, Lisetta Koe (eds.), *Richard Meier. Architect. Volume 4*, New York: Rizzoli, 2004

▶ Harold M. Williams (et alii), *Making Architecture: The Getty Center*, Los Angeles: J. Paul Getty Trust, 1997

Credits

The Author

Philip Jodidio studied art history and economics at Harvard University, and was the Editor-in-Chief of the French art journal *Connaissance des Arts* from 1980–2002. He has published numerous articles and books, including TASCHEN's *Architecture Now!* series, *Building a New Millennium*, and monographs on Tadao Ando, Santiago Calatrava, Norman Foster, Richard Meier, Jean Nouvel, Renzo Piano, and Álvaro Siza.